SOCIAL SPACES

VOLUME 2

SOCIAL SPACES

VOLUME 2

A PICTORIAL REVIEW

First published in Australia in 2003 by
The Images Publishing Group Pty Ltd
ABN 89 059 734 431
6 Bastow Place, Mulgrave, Victoria, 3170, Australia
Telephone: +61 3 9561 5544 Facsimile: +61 3 9561 4860
Email: books@images.com.au
Website: www.imagespublishinggroup.com

The Images Publishing Group Reference Number: 446

National Library of Australia
Cataloguing-in-Publication data

Social Spaces : a pictorial review.

Includes index.
ISBN: 1 876907 62 2 (v. 2).

1. Public architecture. 2. Architecture, Modern – 20th century. (Series : International spaces series).

725

Co-ordinating Editor: Joe Boschetti
Designed by The Graphic Image Studio Pty Ltd, Mulgrave, Australia
Film by Mission Productions Limited
Printed by Everbest Printing Co. Ltd. in Hong Kong/China

IMAGES has included on its website a page for special notices in relation to this and our other publications. Please visit this site: www.imagespublishinggroup.com

CONTENTS

CONFERENCE AND BUSINESS

Nike World Campus
Beaverton, Oregon, USA
Thompson Vaivoda & Associates Architects, Inc.

1 North elevation: building entry
2 View looking north toward campus café

Opposite:
Circulation spine at Tiger Woods Center

Following pages:
Lobby rotunda at Tiger Woods Center looking north to main public entry

Photo credit: Strode Photographic

1

2

STANFORD
HIS DESTINY IS TO
"Tiger" - the future is among
AND PATIENCE. IN
THE MASTERY OF

OUNGEST TO SLAM. THE FIRST TO DOUBLE AS SI SPORTSMAN
HE YEAR. THE ONLY PLAYER FATED TO DOMINATE IN POWER
SEE THE GAME AND THE WORLD GROW TOGETHER. WE SEE
ND WE WAIT FOR WHAT IS BEYOND.

5

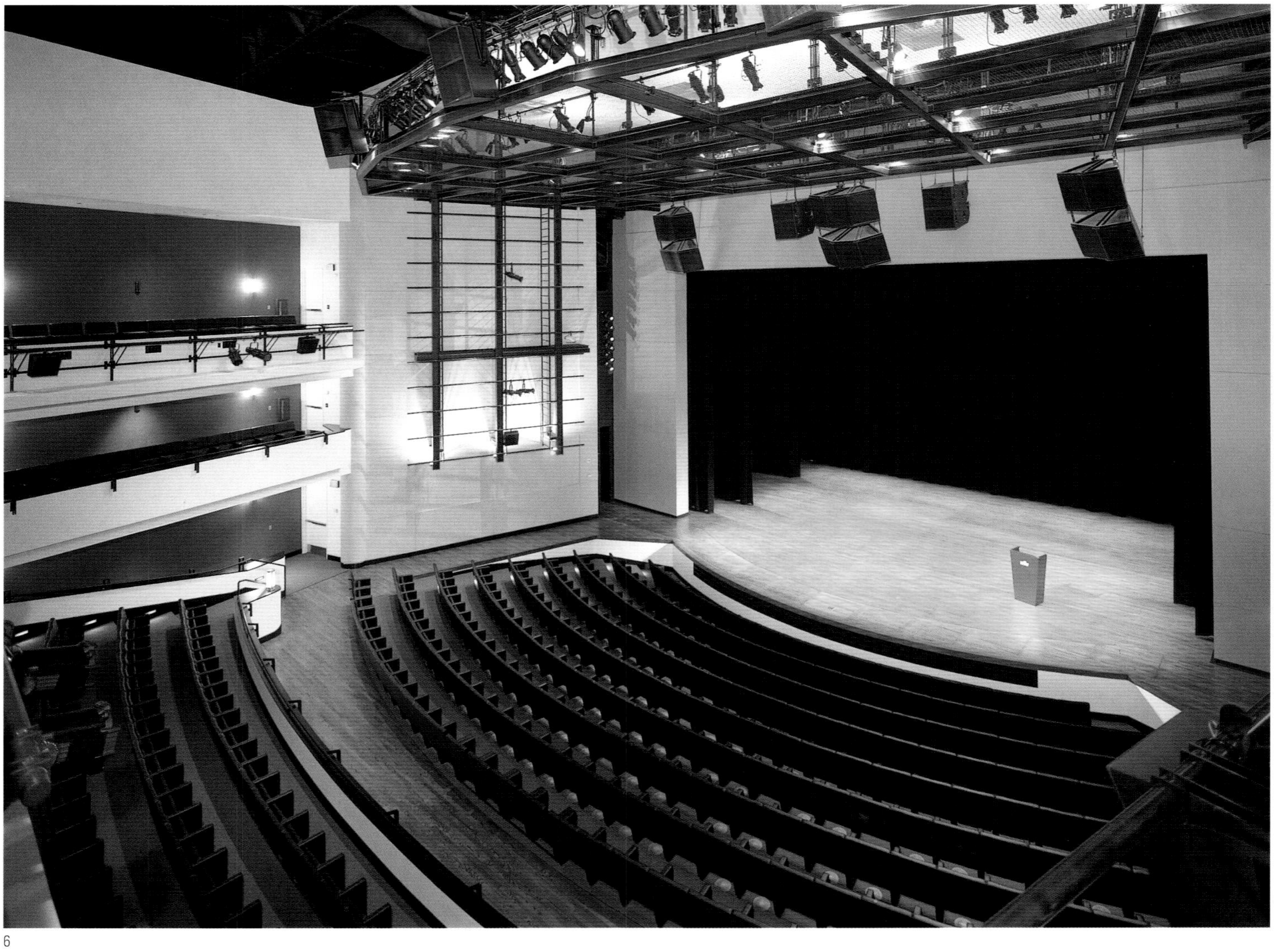

6

Nike World Campus
Beaverton, Oregon, USA
Thompson Vaivoda & Associates Architects, Inc.

5 Campus Design Library in Mia Hamm Center
6 Performing arts theatre in Tiger Woods Center seats 850
7 Lounge seating at Tiger Woods Center
8 Café servery at Mia Hamm Design Center

Photo credit: Strode Photographic

7

8

1

National Wine Centre
Adelaide, South Australia, Australia
Cox Group

1&3 Restaurant and tasting gallery
2 Street view
4 Entry ramp

Photo credit: Trevor Fox

2

3

4

National Wine Centre
Adelaide, South Australia, Australia
Cox Group

5 View into cellars
6 Entrance
7 Entry foyer and ramps

Opposite:
Entrance

Photo credit: Trevor Fox (5–7); Patrick Bingham-Hall (Opposite)

5

6

7

Tickets and Information
Australian Wine Growers Store
Wine Tourism Information
Busby Hall
de Castella's
Kelly's
Broughton's
Fergusson's

Historic 18th & Vine District
Kansas City, Missouri, USA
GouldEvans

1 Street-front exterior
2 Lobby, circulation and performance space
3 Exterior, main museum building façade
4 Jazz museum reception/ticket area

Photo credit: Mike Sinclair

1

2

3

Music is your own experience,
thoughts,
your wisdom,
If you don't live it,

4

ELNORA'S CAFE
The Other Room
RENDEZVOUS FOR
GOOD DRINKS
FOX'S TAP ROOM
New Orleans ROOM
Miltons
TAP ROOM
Lester Young Co.

5

6

7

8

Historic 18th & Vine District
Kansas City, Missouri, USA
GouldEvans

5 Historic signage display
6 Jazz museum exhibits
7 Jazz museum interactive exhibits
8 Stairwell to administration offices

Photo credit: Mike Sinclair

Tribune Interactive
Chicago, Illinois, USA
Perkins & Will
Opposite:
Cross-section of conference room in tower

2 Atrium entrance
3 Corner view of tower conference rooms
4 Tower/floor overview
Photo credit: Hedrich-Blessing

2

3

4

1

FX Centre
Babelsberg, Germany
Harper Mackay Architects

1 Cinemas reflecting scale and grandeur of golden age are part of Europe's first fully integrated digital production centre to service creative media community
2 Public café on upper floor

Photoc credit: Chris Gascoigne Photography

Consular Department Building
Bangkok, Thailand
SJA 3D Co., Ltd.

3 Detail of main approach from street. Walkway is to right of picture
4 General view from northeast with main entrance facing street to north. 20,000-square-metre building on three floors designed to process up to 3,000 passport applications per day
5 Interior view of one of halls for processing passports
6 Night view

Photo credit: courtesy SJA 3D Co., Ltd

2

3

4

5

6

1

2

3

Royal Military Academy Conference Centre
Brussels, Belgium
ASSAR – Teams

1 General view
2 Side corridor
3 Main entrance facing garden plaza
4&6 Main 300-seat auditorium
5 Symposium room with seating for 50

Photo credit: Marc Detiffe

4

5

6

Royal Military Academy Conference Centre
Brussels, Belgium
ASSAR – Teams

7 Vertical circulation

8 Main auditorium

Photo credit: Marc Detiffe

Phoenix Civic Plaza
Phoenix, Arizona, USA
SmithGroup JJR

9 Palms and paving patterns recognising desert setting

10 Christmas season festivities

Photo credit: Bill Timmerman

7

8

9

10

1

2

Executive Briefing Center, Nortel Networks
Raleigh, North Carolina
Centerbrook Architects and Planners

1 'Hub' has floating interactive touch-screen modules for product demonstration
2 Reception hall has visitor registration booths that create digital IDs for visitors

Photo credit: Peter Aaron/Esto

M&C Saatchi Advertising Agency
London, UK
Harper Mackay Architects

3 Entrance – journey through agency begins in square adjacent to entrance
4 Social heart – space of reception becomes continuous with social heart of agency
5 Atrium and glass bridge created over central café area provide focal hub for office
6 Stairs – grand stair continues promenade through agency
7 Office overview – working heart of agency sits next to its social focus
8 Meeting point – openness of entire agency is seen by everyone

Photo credit: Chris Gascoigne Photography

3

4

5

6

7

8

Harbour Town
Gold Coast, Queensland, Australia
Buchan Group

1&3 Harbour Town's wide streets and colourful façades have created a shopping centre with a strong feeling of traditional town centre

2 Signage at Harbour Town is colourful and memorable, with strong links to its Gold Coast location

4 Graphics, signage and pavement treatments bring colour to Harbour Town's streets

Photo credit: Studio Sept

1

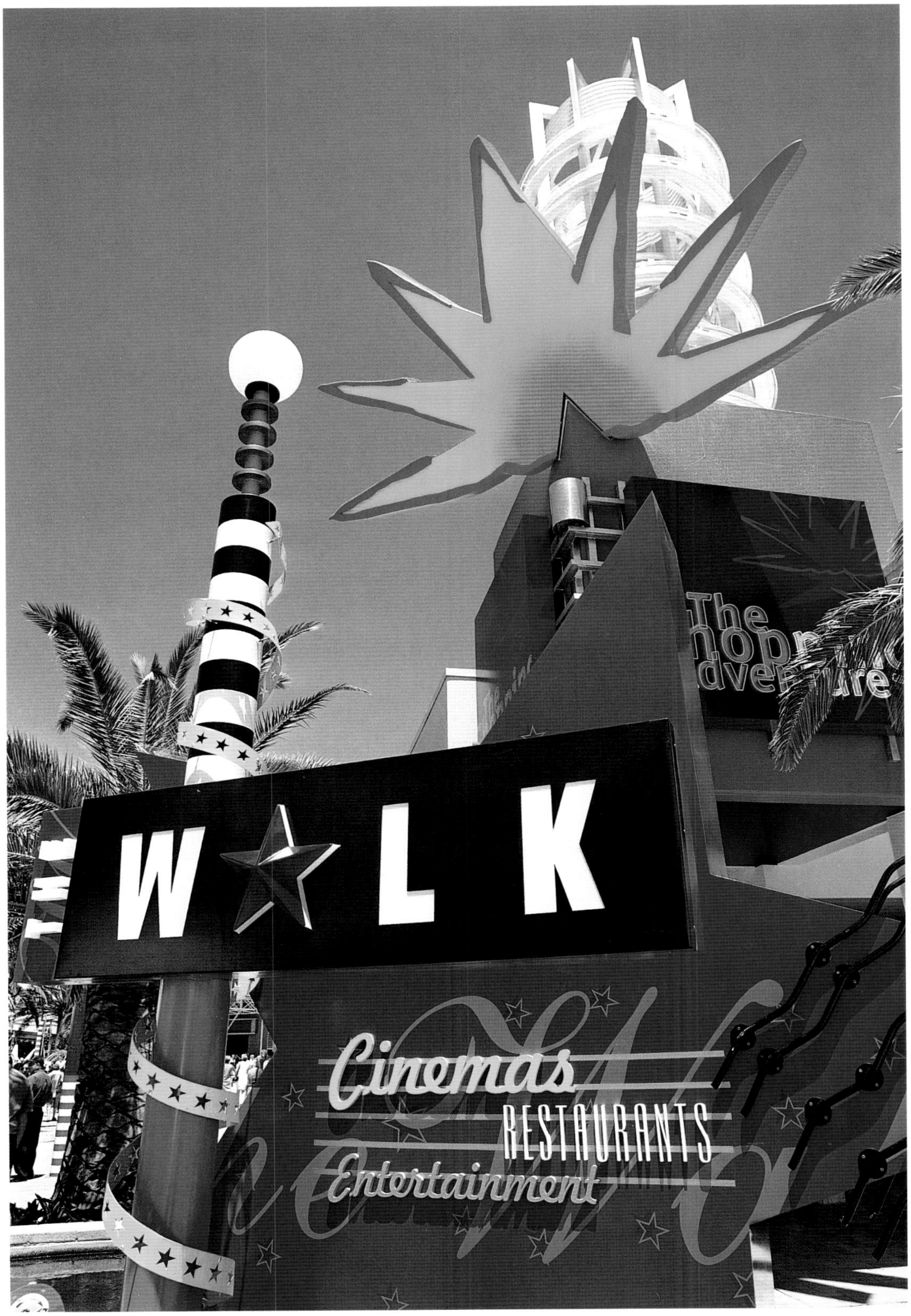

W L K
Cinemas
RESTAURANTS
Entertainment

2

East Carpark
POLO RALPH

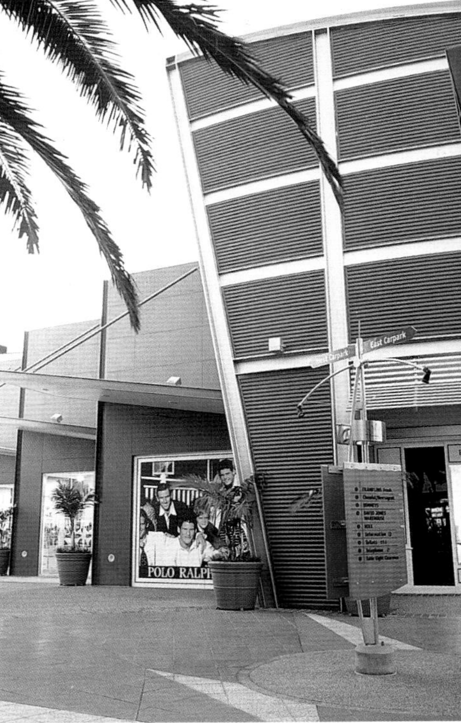

3

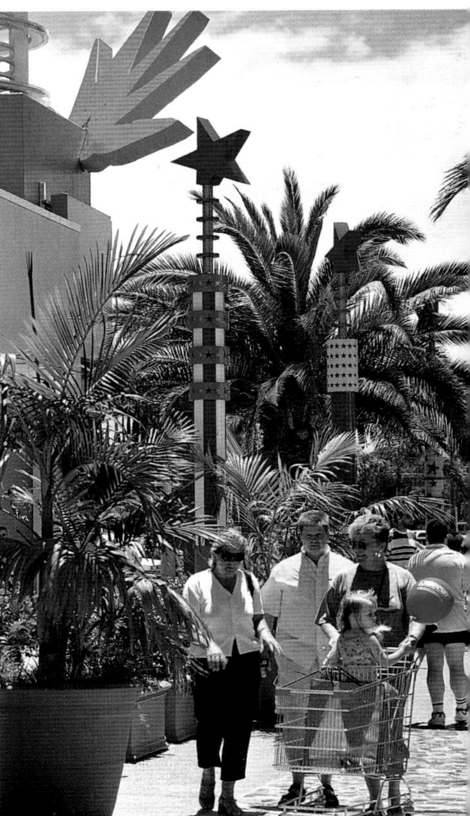

4

5

6

7

Harbour Town
Gold Coast, Queensland, Australia
Buchan Group

5&6 Graphics, signage and pavement treatments bring colour to Harbour Town's streets

7 Sidewalk cafés and open piazza areas enhance the relaxed ambience of Harbour Town

Photo credit: Studio Sept

Valtech Consulting
London, UK
Harper Mackay Architects

1 Café 1: in modern work environments there is a need for a continuous reconfiguration of geometries
2 Bathroom: distortion and deception occurs to spatial boundaries by extending space beyond its surface
3 Café 2: themed zones of each public space is treated as stage set, like café in forest for sitting

Photo credit: Chris Gascoigne Photography

Roanoke Celebration
Roanoke, Virginia, USA
Centerbrook Architects and Planners

4 Roanoke's downtown Market Building and central square were renovated to create a celebration space

Photo credit: courtesy Centerbrook Architects and Planners

Oriental Plaza
Beijing, PRC
P&T Group

5 Main lobby of commercial tower
6 West Plaza
7 Bamboo Island

Photo credit: P&T Group Photographic Department

1

2

3

4

5

6

7

1

2

3

Austin Convention Center
Austin, Texas, USA
Lawrence W. Speck of PageSoutherlandPage

1 Ballroom lobby spills out onto social terraces at creek side
2 Monumental façade on major urban arterial
3 Meeting rooms top deep arcade at major entry point
4 'Board room' pavilion terminates axis of downtown street

Photo credit: Craig D. Blackmon (1&2); Richard Payne, FAIA, Architectural Photographer (4)

4

Austin Convention Center
Austin, Texas, USA
Lawrence W. Speck of PageSoutherlandPage

5 Dramatic downtown view framed by boardroom window

Opposite:
Rotunda makes grand transition from street level to ballroom

Photo credit: Richard Payne, FAIA, Architectural Photographer

5

A
PERFECT
URDER
COMING SOON

CINEMAS, THEATRES AND ENTERTAINMENT

Kurayoshi Park Square
Tottori, Japan
Cesar Pelli & Associates in association with Jun Mitsui

1 Overview

2 Main entrance

Opposite:
Passenger elevator in atrium

Photo credit: Naoomi Kurozumi

1

2

5

6

7

8

Kurayoshi Park Square
Tottori, Japan
Cesar Pelli & Associates in association with Jun Mitsui

Opposite:
Atrium interior
5&6 Large theatre
7 Small theatre
8 Atrium interior

Photo credit: Naoomi Kurozumi

1

2

3

Westminster Promenade and AMC Theaters
Westminster, Colorado, USA
GouldEvans

1 Exterior of ticket area
2 Theatre interior, view to concession
3 Theatre façade and promenade plaza
4 Theatre with stadium seating
5 Bathroom

Photo credit: Mike Sinclair

4

5

PRIVATE

7

Westminster Promenade and AMC Theaters
Westminster, Colorado, USA
GouldEvans

Opposite:
Theatre interior, gathering space/atrium

Photo credit: Mike Sinclair

Sadler's Wells
Islington, London, UK
Arts Team @ RHWL

7 Main foyer stair rises through exhibition space bringing life and colour to entrance elevation

8 Art Screen introduces events and activities at night

9 Perforated wall linings of performance space allow total transformation of spirit of theatre at each show. Technical galleries on display in this instance

Photo credit: John Walsom

8

9

1

2

3

4

QUT Gardens Theatre
Queensland University of Technology,
Brisbane, Queensland, Australia
Peddle Thorp Architects

1 Main drive
2 Theatre
3 Public amenities
4 Theatre foyer courtyard
5 Auditorium
6 Foyer and courtyard

Photo credit: Grapeshot Studios, Stephen Walker

5

6

1

2

Cinema Multiplex
Prague, Czech Republic
JESTICO + WHILES with ATP

1 External envelope formed by pristine rectilinear box
2 Passageway of curves and angles, bathed in coloured light
3 Auditoria equipped with latest sound and projection systems
4 Rich hues and elliptical planes used in washrooms
5 Spiralling cone-shaped entrance foyer

Photo credit: Ales Jungmann

3

4

5

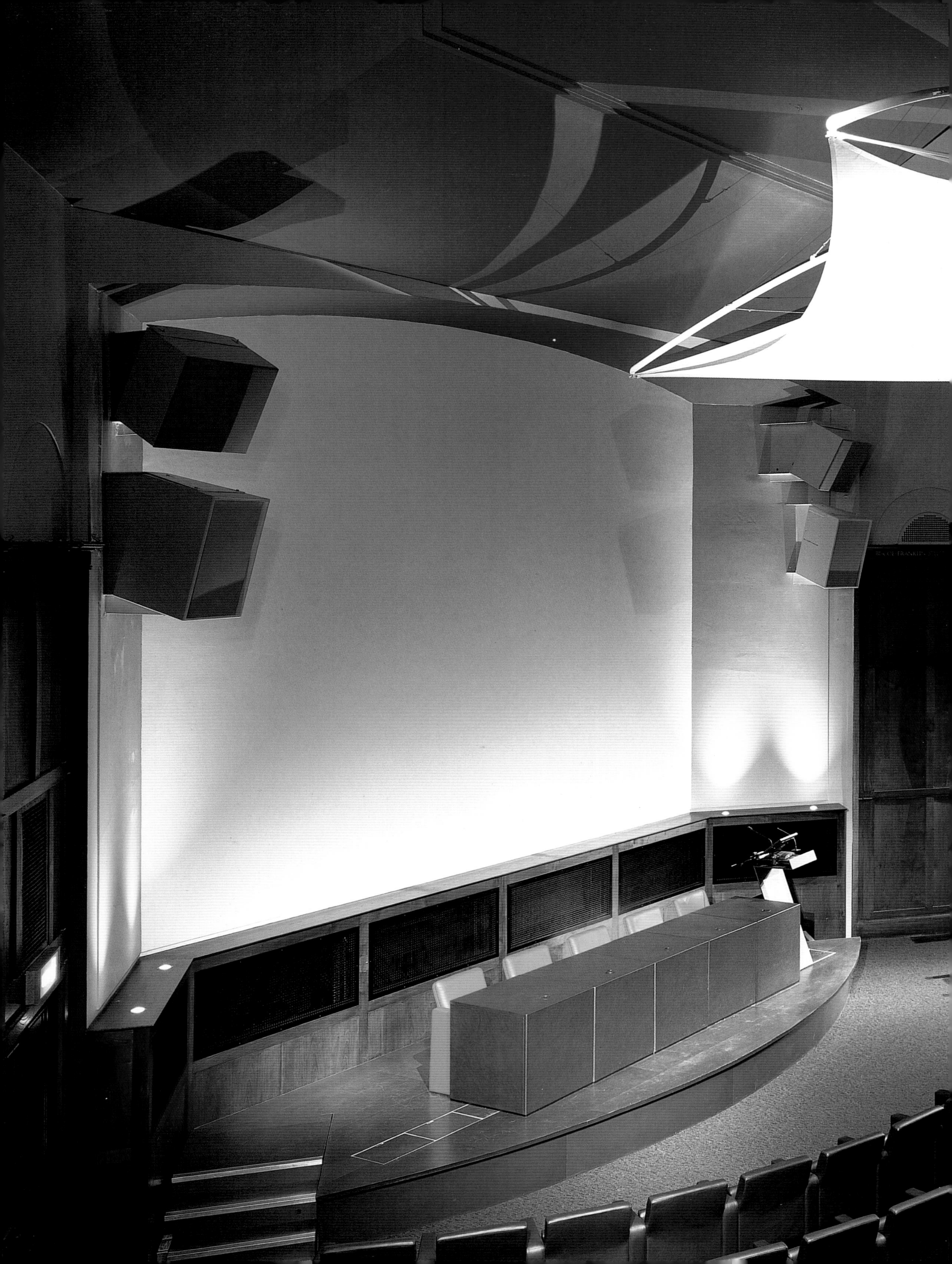

MURCHISON·LIVINGSTONE·BAKER·KIRK
GODWIN AUSTEN·CLARKE·MARKHAM·YULE
STANLEY·DOUGHTY·THOMSON·JOHNSTON
MURRAY·CURZON·SCOTT

2

MURCHISON · LIVINGSTONE · BAKER · KIRK
GODWIN-AUSTEN · CLARKE · MARKHAM · YULE
STANLEY · DOUGHTY · THOMSON · JOHNSTO

3

4

The Ondaatje Theatre
Royal Geographical Society (with IBG), Kensington Gore, London, UK
Studio Downie Architects

Previous pages:
Fabric ceiling – general view
2 Rear stalls/balcony – general view
3 Front stalls – timber panelling
4 Rear stalls – rear walkway

Photo credit: James Morris/Axiom Photographic Agency Ltd

John F Kennedy Center for Performing Arts
Washington, DC, USA
Hartman-Cox Architects

5 Renovated concert hall

Photo credit: Peter Aaron/Esto

5

Montante Cultural Center
Canisius College, Buffalo, New York, USA
Cannon Design

1 View of balcony from newly installed stage

2 Adaptive re-use of former church for performing arts

Opposite:
Main performance hall with seating for 700 attendees

Photo credit: Tim Wilkes Photography

1

2

LIBRARIES, MUSEUMS AND INFORMATION

2

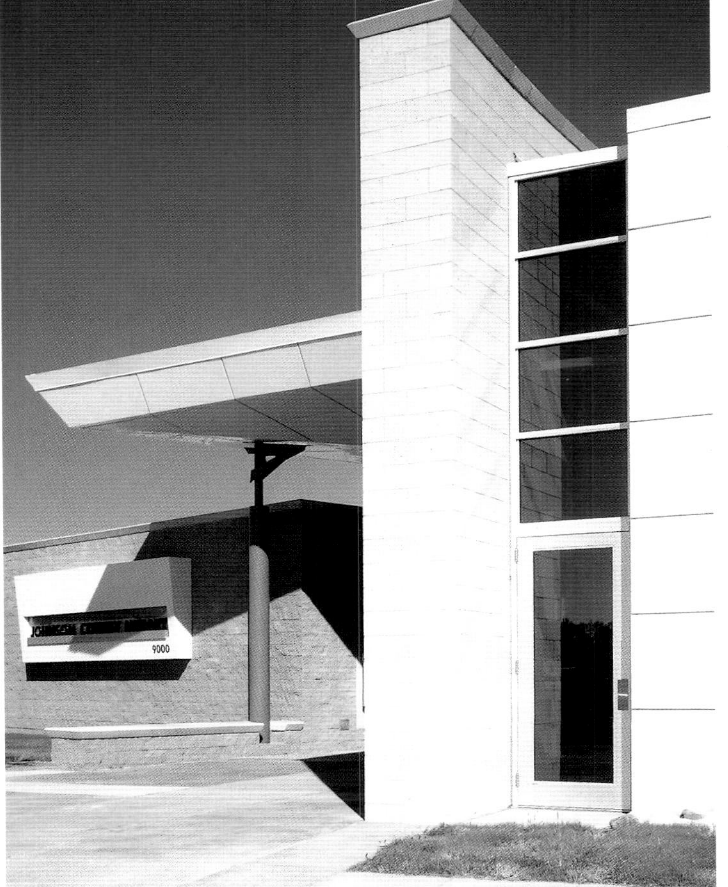

3

4

5

Johnson County Library/Blue Valley
Overland Park, Kansas, USA
GouldEvans

Opposite:
Exterior with native grasses
2 Exterior at night
3 Entry exterior
4 Sunlit library services area
5 Checkout area

Photo credit: Mike Sinclair

1

2

3

Peggy Notebaert Nature Museum
Chicago, Illinois, USA
Perkins & Will

1 View from west
2 Butterfly haven
3 Bird walk and butterfly haven

Photo credit: Steinkamp/Ballogg

Peggy Notebaert Nature Museum
Chicago, Illinois, USA
Perkins & Will

4 Building lobby
5 Butterfly haven

Photo credit: Steinkamp/Ballogg

Art and Art History Building, Colgate University
Hamilton, New York, USA
Centerbrook Architects and Planners

6 Stepped walkway next to building serves as campus path and gathering place
7&8 Spacious lobbies on second and third floors showcase student art

Photo credit: Jeff Goldberg/Esto

4

5

6

7

8

1

2

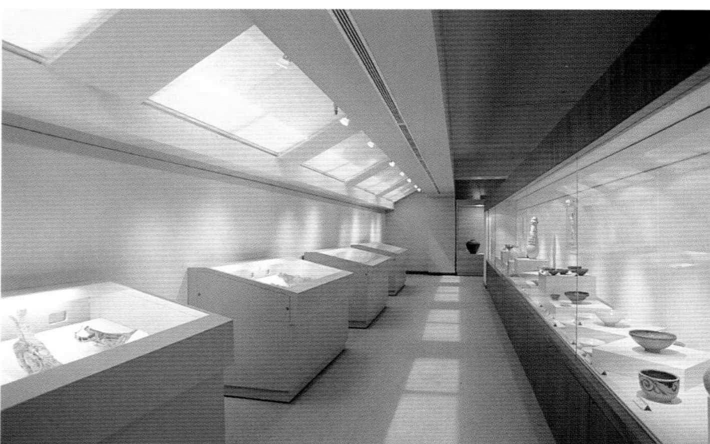

3

4

Founder's Memorial Library
Chinese Cultural University, Taipei, Taiwan
J.J. Pan Architects and Planners with
C.H. Wang, Architect

1 Reading room looking into porch
2 Night view
3 Third-floor museum display
4 Conference hall
5 Fourth-floor museum display
6 Entry plaza from south west
7 Conference hall and museum lobby

Photo credit: Min-Shiung Tsien

5

6

7

QUT Art Museum
Queensland University of Technology, Brisbane, Queensland, Australia
Peddle Thorp Architects

1 Main entrance to gallery
2 Reception and entry foyer
3 Entry foyer and transition ramp
4 Main temporary exhibition gallery
5 Main galleries and sculpture display box

Photo credit: Grapeshot Studios, Stephen Walker

Winterthur Museum
Wilmington, Delaware, USA
Hartman-Cox Architects

6 Addition entrance/atrium

Photo credit: Peter Aaron/Esto

1

2

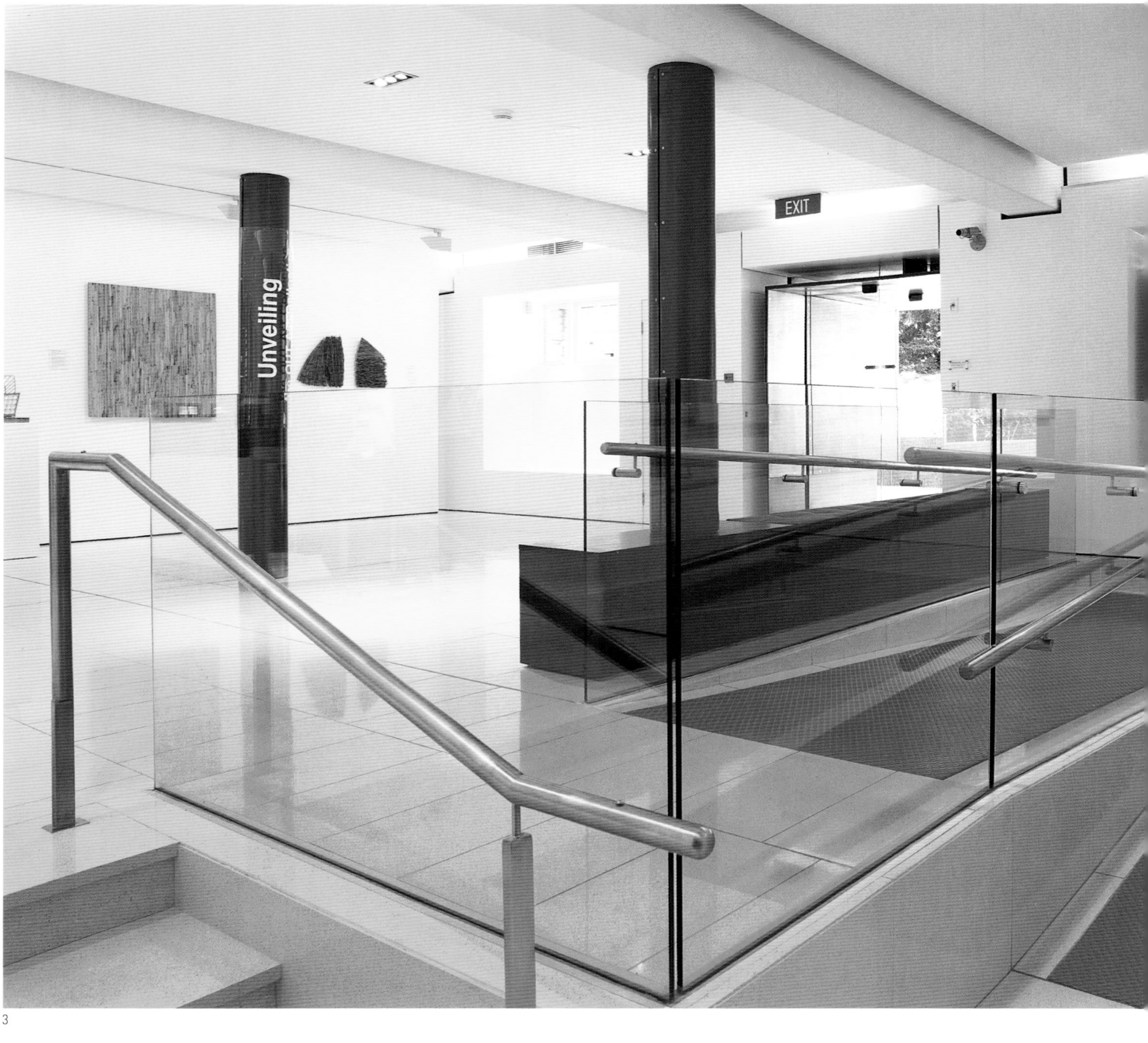

3

4

5

6

Web of North Holland
Haarlemmermeer, The Netherlands
Oosterhuis.nl

1 Interactive red spot inside virtual reality space
2 One of two hydraulically operated entrances
3 Detail of steel construction showing flexible fixtures for hylite panels on steel construction
4 Visitor contemplates next move in interactive space
5 Wide-open gaps in walls make building appear weightless when lit from inside

Photo credit: courtesy the architect (1–4); Tom van Emmerik (5)

Information Café, Homer D. Babbidge Library
University of Connecticut, Storrs, Connecticut, USA
Centerbrook Architects and Planners

6 Workstations in café format encourage students to interact freely in small groups

Photo credit: Robert Benson

1

2

3

4

5

6

Arnold Bernhard Library, Quinnipiac University
Hamden, Connecticut, USA
Centerbrook Architects and Planners

1 Sitting steps at base of library tower also serve as stage for gala events
2 Loft attracts students to its ambience of dappled sunlight
3 Rotunda provides powerful landmark as well as flood of light to which all are drawn
4 Density and sociability of cyber-café attracts students at all times of day and night
5 Team study rooms provide quiet enclaves for work
6 On-line catalogue computers are positioned on edge of main paths, adding sense of vitality and community to library

Photo credit: Jeff Goldberg/Esto

1

2

3

4

5

6

1

2

3

4

5

Stepping Stones Museum for Children
Norwalk, Connecticut, USA
Centerbrook Architects and Planners

1 Outdoor, enclosed lawn, where parents can convene in shade to watch their children at play, transforms into amphitheatre for theatrical events performed in indoor/outdoor theatre
2 Airplane hanger door opens children's theatre up to outdoor amphitheatre
3 Entrance is marked by anthropomorphic tower, to which we have an emphatic response, where letter 'S', repeated in many different ways, can be found in interactive game for children
4 Raised 'Hub' serves as central landmark for visitors as well as viewing platform from which each exhibit room can be seen. Children hop on steeping stones inlaid into carpet
5 At centre of 'Hub', interactive, kinetic machine fascinates children and adults alike

Photo credit: Jeff Goldberg/Esto

1

2

3

Johnson County Central Resource Library
Overland Park, Kansas, USA
GouldEvans

1 Exterior at dusk with signage
2 Entry area with steel truss protective structure
3 Exterior at night

Photo credit: Mike Sinclair

Johnson County Central Resource Library
Overland Park, Kansas, USA
GouldEvans

Opposite:
Reading and study area along building perimeter

5 Multimedia presentation room
6 Research/reference area
7 Primary corridor with steel beams

Photo credit: Mike Sinclair

5

6

7

Wriston Art Center, Lawrence University
Appleton, Wisconsin, USA
Centerbrook Architects and Planners

1 Amphitheatre has human scale, proximity to entrance of existing student centre, and position on edge of major path that draws people to its offerings
2 Passersby get to peer inside to studios and exhibits
3 Amphitheatre is a place to sit at tables and a display sculpture and, on special occasions, a setting for pageantry

Photo credit: Paul Warchol

Butterfly Vivarium
American Museum of Natural History, New York, New York, USA
Perkins Eastman Architects

4 Queuing corridor information graphics
5 Interior of flight spaces
6 View of queuing corridor information displays from inside the flight space
7 View from queuing corridor looking into Butterfly Conservatory
8 The Butterfly Conservatory

Photo credit: courtesy Perkins Eastman Architects

1

2

3

Metamorphosis
Anatomy

4

5

Ecology

6

7

Conservatory
Butterflies

8

Milton Soldani Afonso Library
University of Santo Amaro -
Unisa/Campus II,
São Paulo, Brazil
Carlos Eduardo Rossi

1 Waiting area and reception features wooden balcony with polyurethane paint. Metallic stairway forms tropical lightness with Trachycarpus palm trees in backgrund
2 Multimedia area showing resin polyurethane auto-equalised floor
3 Study area with tables and lighting developed by architect
4 Periodicals area with special lighting for magazines and newspapers. Furniture developed by architect
5 Partial vision of ground level – waiting area and stairway
6 Male toilets with light colour on walls and abstract design on floor

Photo credit: Zezinho Gracindo

1

2

3

4

5

6

1

2

3

Lender School of Business,
Quinnipiac University,
Hamden, Connecticut, USA
Centerbrook Architects and Planners

1 Centre's human scale and south facing sitting wall engage people, while the low profile of building allows alluring majesty of mountain to fill quadrangle

2&3 Team study rooms are arranged along hall with same social success as front porches along street

4 Rotunda is both shelter and landmark for dramatic entrance into campus

Photo credit: Jeff Goldberg/Esto

4

Carver Public Library
Carver, Massachusetts, USA
ARC/Architectural Resources Cambridge, Inc.

Opposite:
Main Reading Room

2 View from atrium into Main Reading Room/Fiction

3 Main entrance: view from Town Green

4 Reference area

5 Children's area

Photo credit: Nick Wheeler/Wheeler Photographics

2

3

4

5

Nauticus, The National Maritime Center
Norfolk, Virginia, USA
Centerbrook Architects and Planners

1 Nauticus sits on pier jutting into Norfolk's Elizabeth River. Riverfront walkway connects it to residential neighbourhoods and downtown Norfolk
2 People mover slopes up gently over two storeys, bringing people to third floor exhibit gallery
3 Entry to museum is from gangplanks over reflecting pools that spill toward river
4 'Wonder Hall' has giant skylight and is filled with Piranesian assortment of people mover, stairs and balconies. It is place that previews many wonders of Nauticus
5 Interactive exhibits on third floor
6 Theatre has moveable screen that rolls into wall at film's end, surprising the audience with harbour view through huge window

Photo credit: Jeff Goldberg/Esto

2

1

3

4

5

6

PLACES FOR WORSHIP

1

2

3

4

5

White Temple
Kyoto, Japan
Takashi Yamaguchi & Associates

1 Night view from shrine
2 Gutter made from frosted glass
3 Approach to White Temple from main gates
4 General view from east
5 General view across lake

Photo credit: courtesy Takashi Yamaguchi & Associates

6

7

White Temple
Kyoto, Japan
Takashi Yamaguchi & Associates

6 Night view from east
7 View towards west
8 Altar with Buddhist image
9 Natural light enters from both sides

Photo credit: courtesy Takashi Yamaguchi & Associates

8

9

Chapel on Venice Farm
Valinhos, São Paulo, Brazil
Décio Tozzi

1&5 Chapel appears to float on water in predawn, misty light
2 Chapel and reflection on lake
3 Close shot of chapel from rear
4 Sacred space – concrete peel, water and cross

Photo credit: Cristiano Mascaro

1

2

3

4

5

Amistad Chapel, United Church of Christ
Cleveland, Ohio, USA
Centerbrook Architects and Planners

1&2 Chapel, located on ground floor of old Ohio Bell Building in downtown Cleveland, connects to life of street and, symbolically, to world

3 Shape of chapel which had to contend with large, existing columns, is oval formed by symbolic glass ceiling and patten of Jerusalem stone floor tiles, meant to enhance sense of community gathered

Photo credit: Jeff Goldberg/Esto

1

2

3

D.I.T.
LIBRARY
MOUNTJOY SQ.

2

3

4

Grace Gospel Centre
Mong-Eng Presbyterian Church, Taichung, Taiwan

J.J. Pan & Partners, Architects and Planners

Opposite:

	Front corner façade
2,3&4	Congregation hall

Photo credit: Min-Shiung Tsien

1

2

3

4

5

6

7

First Presbyterian Church Addition and Renovation
Topeka, Kansas, USA
GouldEvans

1 West elevation, lobby/gathering area addition
2 Chapel entrance
3 Sanctuary
4 East elevation, lobby/gathering area addition
6 Elegant, transparent congregant gathering space
7 Chapel

Photo credit: Michael Spillars

Che Kung Temple
Tai Wai, Shatin, Hong Kong SAR, PRC
Dennis Lau & Ng Chun Man

8 Giant figure of Che Kung
9 Temple chamber
10 Entrance elevation and new temple

Photo credit: Frankie Wong/Frankie Wong and Michael Che Photography

8

9

10

1

2

St Andrew's Anglican Church
Gracemere, Queensland, Australia
Innovarchi

1&2 Entry with generous overhang. Segmented timber portal frame painted to protect from intense tropical sun. Sense of entry enhanced by two-level masonry 'boxes'

3&4 High-level natural ventilation. Translucent sliding glass changes character from intimate to public. Basic wax finish to concrete floor. Stressed-skin plywood ceiling stabilises building and provides elegant finish

5 View from behind sanctuary wall. Simple wax finish is applied to concrete floor

Photo credit: Jon Linkins

4

3

5

1

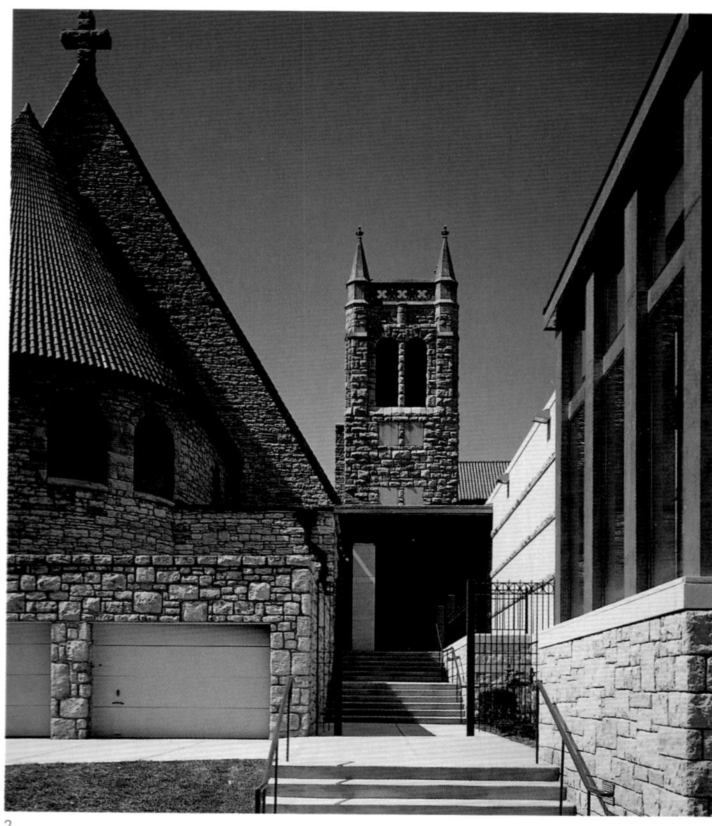
2

3

Grace and Holy Trinity Cathedral
Founders' Hall and Courtyard
Kansas City, Missouri, USA
GouldEvans and Taylor MacDougall Burns

1 Founders' Hall windows from courtyard
2 Intersection of old buildings and new
3 Sanctuary stained glass from courtyard
4 Exterior façade and court
5 Court pergola
6 Founders' Hall

Photo credit: Timothy Hursley

4

5

6

HOSPITALITY AND ACCOMODATION

The Wharf at Woolloomooloo
Woolloomooloo, New South Wales, Australia
Buchan Group

1 Project is enhanced by high quality public spaces and access to waterfront
2 Central atrium
3 Two-level loft suites overlook water

Opposite:
Award-winning redevelopment of the Finger Wharf maximises both the strength of the waterfront location and iconic qualities of heritage-listed wharf buildings

Photo credit: Michael Nicholson

1

2

3

The Wharf at Woolloomooloo
Woolloomooloo, New South Wales, Australia
Buchan Group

5 Central atrium at heart of development serves as transition space, linking public and private uses

6 W Sydney Hotel is located at southern end of wharf. Its 104 rooms, designed by Chhada Siembieda, include 43 loft suites

Photo credit: Michael Nicholson

5

6

1

2

Hakkasan
London, UK
Christian Liagre with JESTICO + WHILES

1 Generously proportioned reception area
2 Atmospherically lit dining spaces
3 Bar of illuminated blue glass and indigenous dark wood
4 China Club, informal lounge area
5 Detail of delicate wood screens and antique panels

Photo credit: Ben Luxmoore

3

4

5

1

2

3

Abacus
Dallas, Texas, USA
edg – Engstrom Design Group

1 Existing building shell was transformed to add depth and interest
2 Vivid colour at the maître d desk
3 Custom railings provide sense of enclosure
4 Geometric design motif is adapted in metal, stone and glass
5 Interiors combine bold architectural features with natural materials

Photo credit: Richard Klein

4

5

Abacus
Dallas, Texas, USA
edg – Engstrom Design Group
6 Open kitchen – elegant, efficient stage for food preparation

Opposite:
Different dining areas radiate from circular entry
Photo credit: Richard Klein

6

King Street Wharf
Sydney, New South Wales, Australia
Cox Group

Opposite:
Promenade

Photo credit: Patrick Bingham-Hall

Star Alliance Lounge
Zurich, Switzerland
Kuwabara Payne McKenna Blumberg Architects

2 Entry at reception
3 Executive class seating area
4 Seating platform in executive class
5 Screened executive class seating area
6 First class seating area

Photo credit: Walter Mair

2

3

4

5

6

1

2

3

Teller's Restaurant
Lawrence, Kansas, USA
GouldEvans

1 Entry and host area
2 Eating areas (mezzanines)
3 Teller 'gates' divide bar from host area; art by Stan Hurd creates a vibrant mural
4 Sculpture, light fixtures, and colour enliven the primary eating area

Photo credit: Mike Sinclair

4

Public Restrooms for People with Disability
São Paulo, Brazil
Antonio Gomes Junior

1. Wash basin made from Italian Nero Marquino marble, designed by the architect
2. Special wood pivot ebony door for entrance to toilet area. An LCD monitor and camera substitute for mirror above the special sink designed for users
3. Visitors welcomed into restroom by seawater aquarium
4. Lighting above marble basin is created by white light filtered by panels of opaque acrylic

Opposite:
General view of entrance to public restroom with focus on seawater aquarium

Photo credit: Martin Szmick

1

2

3

4

Cardwels at the Plaza
Frontenac, Missouri, USA
Suttle Mindlin

1 Upscale restaurant in city's most fashionable shopping centre

Photo credit: Alise O'Brien

Park Hyatt Hotel
Campbell's Cove, Sydney, New South Wales, Australia
Ancher/Mortlock/Woolley - Architects

2 Harbour kitchen bar and restaurant
3 Deli kitchen
4 Chef's table

Photo credit: Park Hyatt, Sales & Marketing

1

2

3

4

Carl Hansen Student Center and Dining Hall, Quinnipiac University
Hamden, Connecticut, USA
Centerbrook Architects and Planners

1 Carved out of existing building and adorned with fanciful places to sit, 'Agora' houses bookstore, bank, post office and convenience store, and is, in effect, 'Town Piazza'

2 Places to sit, no matter how small, add to sociability of centre

Photo credit: Jeff Goldberg/Esto

1

2

Innecto
London, UK
JESTICO + WHILES

1 Main frontage of burnished steel and amber glass
2 Banquette seating of solid walnut
3 Main staircase, clad in raw steel sheeting
4 Main restaurant space

Photo credit: Morley von Sternberg

1

2

3

4

5

6

Innecto
London, UK
JESTICO + WHILES

5 Subterranean cocktail bar
6 Woven strips of American black walnut define space

Photo credit: Morley von Sternberg

Edward Jones YMCA
St Louis, Missouri, USA
Mackey Mitchell Associates

7 Exterior and main lobby of YMCA
8 Lobby with view to weight/training rooms
9 Exterior view into play/daycare area

Photo credit: Sam Fentress

7

8

9

1

2

3

4

5

6

7

Granite Club
Toronto, Ontario, Canada
Kuwabara Payne McKenna Blumberg Architects

1 Member's bar
2 Aperitif bar from formal dining room
3 Member's dining room
4 View along Granite Hall and servery at night
5 Aperitif bar
6 Formal dining room from aperitif bar

Photo credit: Peter Sellar/KLIK

Café, School of Business Administration
University of Connecticut, Storrs, Connecticut, USA
Centerbrook Architects and Planners

7 Café offers informal meeting place for students and faculty and opens to an outdoor courtyard. It is adorned with international flags to celebrate school's global focus

Photo credit: Jeff Goldberg/Esto

2

3

Gaia Restaurant,
Hong Kong, Hong Kong SAR, PR of China
Leigh & Orange Ltd

Opposite:
Oval Room
2 Red Room wall sconce
3 Red Private Dining Room
4 Main dining area

Photo credit: Red Dog Studio

4

1

Caesar Towers Berrini (Blue Towers Hotels)
São Paulo, Brazil
Carlos Bratke Ateliê de Arquitetura

1 General view of building and surroundings
2 Internal view of lobby
3 Front entrance
4 Entrance facing street

Photo credit: Jose Moscardi Jr

2

3

4

1

2

3

Pledger Guest Cabin
West Lake Hills, Texas, USA
Barbee Associates, Inc.

1 View on approach showing cabin and cistern, looking east
2 View to northeast showing cistern, porch, and bath compartment
3 Shutter detail
4 Living room toward sleeping compartments, entry and dining

Photo credit: Paul Bardagjy

4

Pledger Guest Cabin
West Lake Hills, Texas, USA
Barbee Associates, Inc.

5 View to entry showing lighting 'torches'

6 View to northeast

Photo credit: Paul Bardagjy

Renaissance Place
Highland Park, Illinois, USA
Suttle Mindlin

Opposite:
Urban mixed use – apartments and office over upscale retail

Photo credit: Alise O'Brien

5

6

BRENT
BOOKS & CARD
Brent Books &

Marketplace at Sprint International Headquarters Campus
Overland Park, Kansas, USA
GouldEvans

1 Sculptural column at food service entry
2 Inlaid floor and varied ceiling add to festive interior
3 Food service counter

Photo credit: Mike Sinclair

1

2

3

Small Group Housing
Washington University, St Louis, Missouri, USA
Mackey Mitchell Associates

1 Living, eating, dining and social spaces at Small Group Housing
2&3 Informal dining/cafeteria
4 Student Lounge
5 Great Hall
6 Stairwell with seating area

Photo credit: Sam Fentress

1

2

3

4

5

6

1

2

Studium Gegé
São Paulo, Brazil
Fernanda Cunha Bueno

1&3 Stairway to lower-level room with typical interior tropical garden

2 Rear façade showing modernist house built in 1960s and renovated for use as a private business club to provide accommodation to visiting members and guests

4 Corridor with internal tropical garden. Exit to laundry, bedrooms, pantry and kitchen

Photo credit: Luis Antônio Esteves

3

4

Businessmen's Private Club
São Paulo, Brazil
Studium Gegé & Fernanda Cunha Bueno

5 Dining room – wall is focal point with painting based on Dutch painter Rugendas
6&7 Master bedroom and living room
8 General view of living and dining room
9 Library – room used for private meetings features special Brazilian wood wall panels

Photo credit: Luis Antônio Esteves

5

6

7

8

9

1

2

3

St Martins Lane Hotel
London, UK
Harper Mackay Architects with Phillipe Starck

1 Foyer space with carpet of light setting a route map throughout lobby
2 View from outside. Individual control of lighting enables guests to contribute to ever-changing pattern of elevation
3 Entrance lobby, partially viewed through enormous entrance doors
4 Scale and nature are constantly superimposed on experience of hotel
5 Drama and scale of public space is intensified by ever-changing palette of light in bar

Photo credit: Tod Eberle

4

5

1

Westwood Country Club
St Louis, Missouri, USA
Suttle Mindlin

1 Exclusive country club in traditional, yet modern surrounding

Photo credit: Alise O'Brien

Junior League of St Louis
St Louis, Missouri, USA
Mackey Mitchell Associates

2–4 Space for dining, reception and private parties

Photo credit: Cheryl Pendleton

2

3

4

1

2

BleuJacket Restaurant
Lawrence, Kansas, USA
GouldEvans

1 Host station, view toward lounge
2 Lounge area
3 Patron seating, view to bar
4 Exposed beams, stone wall contract with fine fabrics, mesh screen

Photo credit: Mike Sinclair

3

4

1

2

3

Ursa's Café
Washington University, St Louis, Missouri, USA
Mackey Mitchell Associates

1 University dining
2 Student lounge
3 Living, eating, dining and social spaces at Small Group Housing

Photo credit: Barclay Goeppner

The Barbary Coast Supper Club
San Francisco, California, USA
Inglese Architecture/ISTUDIOS

4 Club Blue Room
5 Club bar
6 Club dining and dance platform

Photo credit: Jay Cunanan

4

5

6

1

Majestic Café
Alexandria, Virginia, USA
McInturff Architects

1 Front façade with restored neon
2 Dining room viewed from entry
3 Bar and front counter seating

Photo credit: Julia Heine

2

3

Majestic Café
Alexandria, Virginia, USA
McInturff Architects

4 Detail of banquette and wait station
5 Dining room with bar beyond
6 Dining room banquette with skylights above

Photo credit: Julia Heine

4

5

6

PLAYGROUNDS AND GYMNASIA SPACES

Kilpatrick Athletic Center
Simon's Rock College of Bard, Great Barrington, Massachusetts, USA
Centerbrook Architects and Planners

1 Athletic Center forms main gateway to campus, conveying rusticity of Berkshires

2 Juice bar is campus gathering place

Opposite:
Upper lobby uses wood, natural light and soaring spaces to inspire athletes

Photo credit: Steve Rosenthal

1

2

4

5

6

Kilpatrick Athletic Center
Simon's Rock College of Bard, Great Barrington, Massachusetts, USA
Centerbrook Architects and Planners

4 Climbing wall, with windows that afford views from other spaces

5 Structure over pool is southern yellow pine laminated trusses supporting southern yellow pine decking

6 Squash courts open to two-storey space that allows passersby to watch

7 Twenty-five yard pool washed in diffused natural light

Photo credit: Steve Rosenthal

7

Hyogo Prefectural Tajima Dome
Hyogo Prefecture, Japan
Mitsuru Senda + Environment Design Institute

1&3 Baseball game with roof closed
2 View of east side with open dome
4 Entrance hall
5 Environment discovery play structures laid out in two rows of 1.8-metres by 1.8-metres
6 Third floor of sports museum

Photo credit: Mitsumasa Fujitsuka

1

2

3

4

5

6

Princess Diana Memorial Playground
London, UK
JESTICO + WHILES

1 Entrance doors, etched with child-height figures
2 'Home under the ground' under a soft landscaped mound
3 Three truncated cones direct sunlight into space beneath

Photo credit: James Morris

1

2

3

4

5

6

Princess Diana Memorial Playground
London, UK
JESTICO + WHILES

4 Wash basins derived from JM Barrie's 'Never Tree'

Photo credit: James Morris

Far Oaks Golf Club
Fairview Heights, Illinois, USA
Mackey Mitchell Associates

5–7 Indoor dining or front porch relaxation

Photo credit: Sam Fentress

7

1

2

3

4

5

Kainan Wanpaku Park
Kainan City, Wakayama Prefecture, Japan
Mitsuru Senda + Environment Design Institute

1 View from Wind Hill to Kazenoko building. Families enjoy grass skiing on holidays

2&3 'Wind Corridor' extends from Kazenoko building, and continues 300 metres to woods to symbolise development of play

4 Spiral net equipment – view looking up

5 Three-dimensional Tornado connected by spiral net to child elevator

6 Interior of Kazenoko theatre – view looking up

7 'Jump' is designed for five or six-year old-children

8 Wind corridor play equipment and colourful FRP tubes

Photo credit: Mitsuru Senda (1); Mitsumasa Fujitsuka (2–8)

6

7

8

EXIT
EXIT

Orange Coast College Art Center
Costa Mesa, California, USA
Steven Ehrlich Architects

5–7 Three-storey atrium connects this multidisciplinary facility

Photo credit: Adrian Velicescu

New Student Center
St Mary's College of Maryland,
St Mary's City, Maryland, USA
Hartman-Cox Architects

8 New dining hall

Photo credit: Robert Lautman

5

6

7

8

1

Perrysburg High School
Perrysburg, Ohio, USA
Fanning/Howey Associates, Inc.

1 Variety of cafeteria seating options
2 Stair landing designed to serve as podium for speakers
3 Cafeteria/commons serves as a public lobby/concession area
4 Natural light is provided by translucent skylight over cafeteria/commons

Photo credit: Emery Photography, Inc.

2

3

4

1

2

4

3

Pratt Center
Long Island University, Brooklyn, New York, USA
Mitchell/Giurgola Architects, LLP

1 Façade
2 Third-floor lounge
3 Entrance to Pratt Center off Pedestrian Esplanade

Photo credit: Jeff Goldberg/Esto

Zeckendorf Building
Long Island University, Brooklyn, New York, USA
Mitchell/Giurgola Architects, LLP

4 First-floor atrium
5 Pedestrian Esplanade and entrance to Pratt Center

Photo credit: Jeff Goldberg/Esto

5

Linguan University
TUEN MUN, Hong Kong, PRC
P&T Group
1 Main entrance
2&3 Typical academic building
Opposite:
Contemporary chinese garden
Photo credit: P&T Photographic Department

1

2

3

2

3

QUT Childcare Centre
Queensland University of Technology, Brisbane, Queensland, Australia
Peddle Thorp Architects

Opposite:
Main corridor
2 Staff base
3 Child entry doors

Photo credit: Grapeshot Studios, Stephen Walker

1

2

3

International Terminal
O'Hare International Airport,
Chicago, Illinois, USA
Perkins & Will

1 Detail
2 View from tarmac
3 Dusk view of international terminal
4 View of control tower
5 View of gate entry

Photo credit: Hedrich-Blessing

4

5

6

International Terminal
O'Hare International Airport, Chicago, Illinois, USA
Perkins & Will

6 Concourse

Photo credit: Hedrich-Blessing

Barry-Wehmiller Plaza
Clayton, Missouri, USA
Mackey Mitchell Associates

7&8 Renovated city buildings connected by outdoor plaza

Photo credit: Alise O'Brien

Mercantile Plaza
St Louis, Missouri, USA
Mackey Mitchell Associates

9–11 Public plaza in heart of downtown St Louis

Photo credit: Sam Fentress

7

8

10

9

11

Chesterton High School
Chesterton, Indiana, USA
Fanning/Howey Associates, Inc.

1 Chesterton High School main lobby
2 Main entrance of 48,000-square-metre building
3 Checkout desk with great visibility
4 4,000-square-metre Media Center is building heart
5 Warm and inviting student reading and research area

Photo credit: Emery Photography, Inc.

1

2

3

4

5

Children's Court of Victoria
Melbourne, Victoria, Australia
Bates Smart Pty Ltd

1 Little Lonsdale Street entry façade
2 West elevation and through-city block pedestrian way
3 Internal 'street' circulation gallery and Magistrates' bridges
4 Little Lonsdale Street entry façade at night
5 Internal 'street' circulation to courtrooms – artwork by Bruno Leti

Photo credit: John Gollings

1

4

2

3

5

COURT 8

1

2

3

4

5

School of Law Center
Quinnipiac University, Hamden, Connecticut, USA
Centerbrook Architects and Planners

1&4 Outdoor café is positioned immediately on edge of major entry path to centre where people can sit and watch world go by

2 Places to study located near heavily trafficked routes have allure

3 Main lobby has both active public places to gather, and removed, intimate places from which to observe

5 Many places for impromptu interaction are dispersed throughout, each with its own appealing ambience

Photo credit: Jeff Goldberg/Esto

Marion McCain Arts & Social Sciences Building
Dalhousie University, Halifax, Nova Scotia, Canada
Diamond and Schmitt Architects Incorporated

Opposite & 4:
Departmental stairs
2 Graduate lounge with sunscreen
3 Naturally lit oval lecture room

Photo credit: Steven Evans

2

3

4

BIOGRAPHIES

ARC/Architectural Resources Cambridge, Inc.

Founded in 1969, ARC/Architectural Resources Cambridge, Inc. is a fully integrated architectural design firm, providing services in the fields of architecture, planning, programming and interior design, including feasibility analyses, land-use planning, site design, master planning, programming, building design, construction documentation and administration, as well as space planning, furnishing and equipment selection.

The firm has designed various social spaces including campus centres, meeting/conference facilities, student commons and forums for both academic and corporate clients. ARC's higher education clients include Boston College, Boston University, Duke, Harvard, Princeton, Syracuse and Tufts, as well as state universities in Colorado, Iowa, Massachusetts and Missouri. In addition to the public schools designed by the firm, ARC has also provided services to many of the top eastern independent schools; among them are Berkshire, Deerfield, Hotchkiss, Mercersburg, Milton Academy, St. George's and St. Paul's. Clients in the corporate sector include Abbott Labs, Bayer Diagnostics, EMD Pharmaceuticals, Millipore and Genzyme Corporation.

Based in Cambridge, Massachusetts, the firm has a staff of 60 professionals. Nationally recognised for excellence in architecture, ARC/Architectural Resources Cambridge, Inc. has received numerous awards from the American Institute of Architects and other professional organisations. Additional information can be found at www.arcusa.com.

ARC/Architectural Resources Cambridge, Inc.
140 Mount Auburn Street
Cambridge, Massachusetts, USA
Telephone: +1 617 547 2200
Facsimile: +1 617 547 7222
www.arcusa.com

Barbee Associates Inc.

William C. Barbee is the principal architect at Barbee Associates, Inc., an award-winning architecture, interior architecture and preservation firm practicing in Austin, Texas, USA. Project types include banks, hospitality, retail and fitness centres, in addition to their residential and ranching headquarters projects. Most recent awards include the 2002 Texas Society of Architects Design Award, the AIA Austin 2002 Honor Award, and the AIA Western Homes Design Award.

William Barbee's academic career includes a Visiting Assistant Professorship at Texas A&M University, Lecturer at The University of Texas at Austin and at San Antonio, and Assistant Professor in Graduate Studies at The University of Texas at San Antonio.

William Barbee has conducted independent studies in the documentation of historic structures, including the Pueblitos of Dinetah in New Mexico, and the Southern Chacoan Outliers at Chaco Canyon, New Mexico. His studio won the coveted Charles E. Peterson Prize in 1999 from the Historic American Buildings Survey. He also received the 1999 Kenneth L. Anderson Prize from the National Park Service.

Barbee graduated with honours from the University of Texas at Austin with a Bachelor of Arts in Natural Sciences/Pre-Medical in 1973, and a Master of Arts in Biomedical Science from the University of Texas Medical Branch at Galveston in 1975. He entered the New York School of Interior Design where he studied under Giuseppe Zambonini, Michael Kahill and George Ranali. He received a Masters of Architecture from the University of Texas at Austin in 1981.

Barbee Associates Inc.
1201 West 24th Street, Suite 100
Austin, Texas, USA
Telephone: +1 512 494 1201
Facsimile: +1 512 494 1219
www.barbeeinc.com

Carlos Bratke Ateliê de arquitetura

Carlos Bratke has had a long and respected career in architecture and remains a leading figure in architecture in South America. In his prestigious academic career, he has held the positions of Professor of Architecture at both Mackenzie University and Beles Artes University.

As an active figure among the Brazilian architectural community, he was São Paulo divisional president of the Brazilian Institute of Architects, and director of the Museum of Brazilian Housing from 1992–95. He was president of the São Paulo Biennale Foundation from 1999–2002.

Carlos Bratke established his self-titled practice in 1968, and in that time has designed over 300 commercial and industrial buildings, retail centres, hotels, places for worship, schools, cultural centres and houses.

The work of Carlos Bratke features prominently in IMAGES' International Spaces Series and Details in Architecture Series.

Bratke has been highly awarded for his achievements, including the Grand Prize in 1997 of the Third International Biennial of Architecture of São Paulo, the Vitrubio Award of the National Museum of Beunos Aires, the 1997 Brazilian Congress of Architects Curitiba Prize for his life's work, the Rino Levi Annual Award from the São Paulo division of the Brazilian Institute of Architects in 1985, and the Paulista Salon of Fine Arts Award (Architecture) 1979, 1981, 1983.

Bratke's international projects have been built in the USA, Uruguay, Mexico and Israel.

Carlos Bratke Ateliê de arquitetura
Av. Eng. Luiz Carlos Berrini, 1091 – 20 Andar
Brooklin Novo – 04571-010
São Paulo, Brazil
Telephone: +55 11 5505 2344
Facsimile: +55 11 5505 2232
www.arquitetura.com.br/bratke

Cannon Design

Founded over 50 years ago, Cannon Design is an internationally ranked multidisciplinary firm of 500, recognised for design excellence and technological innovation, and known for performance and dedication to client service. A 'single firm, multi-office' practice approach enables the firm to focus on the resources of its staff to meet client needs through a network of 10 regional offices nationwide.

By assembling all disciplines within the organisation, a committed team of architects, engineers, planners and interior designers, offers clients a single point of responsibility and accountability, ensuring each project's success.

Cannon Design is focused upon developing long-term relationships with its clients, based upon the trust earned through performance. The firm strives to create environments that are a thoughtful response to the programme mission, physical setting and functional purpose, reflecting the spirit and personality of each owner.

Cannon Design has defined its mission clearly with a focus on quality – with client satisfaction as the ultimate measurement. As a leader in quality, Cannon Design works continuously to advance the state of the art, contributing to the built environment and quality of life of the people for whom living and working spaces are created.

Cannon Design
2170 Whitehaven Road
Grand Island, New York, USA
Telephone: +1 716 773 6800
Facsimile: +1 716 773 5909
www.cannondesign.com

INDEX

IMAGES is pleased to add 'Social Spaces, Volume 2' to its compendium of design and architectural publications.

We wish to thank all participating firms for their valuable contribution to this publication and especially the following firms who provided photographs for the divider pages:

Conference and Business

Thompson Vaivoda & Associates Architects, Inc.

Photo credit: Strode Photographic

Cinemas, Theatres and Entertainment

GouldEvans

Photo credit: Mike Sinclair

Libraries, Media Centres and Museums

ARC/Architectural Resources Cambridge, Inc.

Photo credit: Nick Wheeler/Wheeler Photographics

Places For Worship

Centerbrook Architects and Planners

Photo credit: Jeff Goldberg/Esto

Hospitality and Accommodation

Jestico + Whiles

Photo credit: Ben Luxmoore

Playgrounds and Gymnasia Spaces

Centerbrook Architects and Planners

Photo credit: Jeff Goldberg/Esto

Other

Centerbrook Architects and Planners

Photo credit: Jeff Goldberg/Esto

We gratefully acknowledge the St Martins Lane Hotel for granting special permission for the use of their photographs in this book.

The St Martins Lane Hotel featured on pages 156-57 is located at:
St Martins Lane Hotel
45 St Martins Lane
London WC2 UK
Tel: +44 (0)20 7300 5500
www.ianschragerhotels.com